THE ASCENSION DIMENSION OFFICIAL WORKBOOK

EXERCISING KINGDOM AUTHORITY TO TRIUMPH OVER CIRCUMSTANCES AND OPPOSITION

ISAAC PITRE

DESTINY IMAGE

Destiny Image P.O. Box 310, Shippensburg, PA 17257-0310

This book and all other Destiny Image's books are available at Christian bookstores and distributors worldwide.

For Worldwide Distribution.

Reach us on the Internet: www.destinyimage.com.

ISBN 13 TP: 9798881504380

ISBN 13 eBook: 9798881504397

CONTENTS

INTRODUCTION

Welcome to **The Ascension Dimension Official Workbook**—a life-changing guide to help you unlock the power, authority, and purpose of living in the ascended life with Christ. This workbook is designed to take deep spiritual truths and make them practical for your everyday life, empowering you to experience all that God has promised.

The ascension of Jesus is a cornerstone of our faith, but many believers struggle to understand its full impact on their lives. Through this workbook, you will learn how to live from your position in heavenly places, walking in the victory, authority, and freedom that Jesus secured for you. This journey is not reserved for a select few—it's an invitation for every believer to experience the fullness of life in Christ.

WHAT YOU WILL LEARN

- **Your New Position in Christ** One of the most important truths you'll uncover is that your spiritual position is not based on your earthly circumstances. You have been raised with Christ and seated in heavenly places. This means you live from a place of victory, not striving for it. As you embrace this reality, you will learn to overcome fear, doubt, and defeat.

- **The Role of the Holy Spirit** The Holy Spirit is your guide, teacher, and source of strength in this journey. This workbook will show you how to partner with the Spirit to access God's wisdom, power, and direction. Through His guidance, you'll discover how to live beyond natural limits and step into the supernatural.

- **Exercising Authority and Dominion** Jesus's ascension placed Him above all things, and as His co-heir, you share in that authority. This workbook will teach you how to exercise spiritual dominion, overcome the enemy, and speak life into your circumstances. You'll learn practical steps to walk in the authority Jesus has given you.

- **Fulfilling Kingdom Purpose** Living in the ascension dimension isn't just about personal blessings; it's about advancing God's Kingdom. This workbook will challenge you to align your life with God's purposes, teaching you how to bring heaven's realities into your world. Whether through prayer, acts of love, or sharing your faith, you'll be equipped to make an eternal impact.

- **The Power of Prayer and Declarations** Prayer is one of your greatest tools for releasing God's power on earth. This workbook will help you develop a deeper prayer life, showing you how to partner with God to bring His will into reality. You'll also learn how to make declarations that align with His Word, unleashing the power of your faith-filled words.

- **Walking in Love and Spiritual Maturity** Love is the foundation of ascension living. Without it, spiritual power loses its impact. This workbook will guide you in cultivating forgiveness, walking in peace, and reflecting Christ's love in every area of your life. As you grow in love, you'll see greater unity, strength, and effectiveness in your faith.
- **Practical Application for Daily Life** The ascension dimension isn't just a theological concept; it's a way of life. Through reflective questions, action steps, and journaling prompts, this workbook will help you apply what you've learned to your daily challenges and relationships. You'll discover how to live victoriously in every area of your life.

WHAT TO EXPECT

This workbook is structured to make the principles of ascension living clear, practical, and actionable. Each chapter is designed to deepen your understanding and help you apply these truths. Here's what you can expect in each section:

- **10 Key Points Summary:** A clear and detailed explanation of the chapter's main lessons.
- **Reflective Questions:** Thoughtful prompts to help you process and apply the material.
- **Actionable Steps:** Practical ways to cultivate, equip, and engage with ascension truths.
- **Words of Encouragement and Scripture:** Uplifting reminders from God's Word to inspire and strengthen you.

- **Journaling Prompts:** Guided exercises to help you personalize and internalize the lessons.

BY THE END OF THIS WORKBOOK, YOU WILL:

- Understand your identity and inheritance in Christ.
- Walk confidently in the power of the Holy Spirit.
- Overcome spiritual challenges with faith and authority.
- Align your life with God's Kingdom purpose.
- Experience the fullness of God's promises in your daily life.

A JOURNEY OF TRANSFORMATION

The ascension dimension is not just an idea—it's a reality that can transform how you live, think, and interact with the world. As you work through this book, you'll be challenged to change old mindsets, embrace deeper faith, and step into supernatural living.

This is your moment to take hold of all that God has for you. Whether you're new to faith or have walked with Christ for years, this workbook is your tool for growth and empowerment. You'll uncover the practical truths that will help you live as a child of God, equipped to overcome challenges and bring heaven's realities into your world.

The journey ahead will require focus, commitment, and an open heart. But as you press into these truths, expect to see God move powerfully in your life. He has already raised you up and seated you with Christ in heavenly places. Now it's time to live from that position and let His power flow through you.

AN INVITATION TO ASCENSION LIVING

Through this workbook, you'll not only understand the ascension dimension but also live it out. This is more than a study guide—it's a tool for transformation. As you engage with the chapters, you'll discover the full potential of your identity in Christ and the limitless possibilities of a Spirit-filled life.

Remember, this journey is not about striving but about receiving. Jesus has already accomplished the work. Your role is to believe, embrace, and live in the reality of His finished work. With the Holy Spirit as your guide, you have everything you need to step into this dimension of faith, power, and purpose.

Welcome to the ascension life. Let's begin this journey together. Your breakthrough is waiting, and your destiny in Christ is within reach.

~

CHAPTER 1
THE REST OF THE STORY PHASE

Be encouraged that your salvation is not just about escaping sin but entering into a dynamic and powerful life with Christ. You are raised and seated with Him, which changes everything about how you should view your life and mission on earth.

Ephesians 2:6 (NKJV): "and raised us up together, and made us sit together in the heavenly places in Christ Jesus,"

As we journey through the gospel message, we often emphasize the death, burial, and resurrection of Jesus Christ, which are undeniably foundational to our faith. However, this perspective is somewhat **incomplete** because it misses another critical phase—the ascension. The ascension of Jesus is not merely a postscript to His resurrection but is central to understanding the full scope of redemption. It is here, as Jesus ascends and takes His seat at the right hand of the Father, that the works of salvation find their true **consummation**. This event marks the moment when Jesus' earthly mission transitions into His heavenly ministry, signifying the completion of His redemptive work.

This ascension is pivotal because it symbolizes Jesus not only as a risen savior but as a reigning king. Through the ascension, we, as believers, are invited to **participate in Christ's phases** of death, burial, resurrection, and ascension through our own spiritual experiences. When we accept Christ, we are not merely acknowledging historical facts; we are spiritually entering into these phases ourselves. This is vividly portrayed through our baptism, which symbolizes our death to sin and resurrection to a new life in Christ—a life that is also meant to **ascend** in spiritual maturity and authority.

This participation extends beyond mere symbols; it represents a real, lived experience of **spiritual death and resurrection**. Our old sin nature, inherited from Adam's transgression, is put to death, and we are raised to a new life. This is the spiritual death that Paul talks about—a transformation so profound that it can only be likened to being raised from the dead. It's not about dying physically with Christ but dying to our old sinful selves.

In this new life, we share in the **authority of Jesus**—an authority that He declared having over death and hell. The 'keys' of death and Hades, as mentioned in Revelation, symbolize this authority. Jesus didn't just overcome death for Himself; He overcame it on our behalf. This authority over death isn't confined to the physical raising from the dead, which Jesus demonstrated several times before the cross, but it's primarily about our spiritual resurrection.

Perhaps one of the most transformative aspects of Jesus' work is that as believers, we are **seated with Christ** in the heavenly realms. This isn't just a theological concept to be admired from a distance but a present reality that affects how we live today. Being seated with Christ places us in a position of authority where we operate from heaven's perspective, far above principalities and powers. This position empowers us to live victoriously over sin and to manifest the kingdom of heaven on earth.

Understanding our new position also helps in our **transformation through ascension**. We are not merely saved from sin; we are elevated to sit with Christ in heavenly places. This ascension into spiritual realms is where our perspective shifts from earthly to heavenly, enabling us to see and operate in the reality of the Kingdom of God. It is in recognizing this that we fully grasp the victory and dominion that are ours in Christ.

Jesus' intention in all of this was not solely to redeem us from sin but to bring us into a place of shared glory and power. His desire for us to reign with Him reveals His heart for His followers —we are to be more than servants; we are called to be kings and priests. Thus, the **Christ's desire for believers** is that we do not just look to Him but also join Him in His ongoing work of redemption and kingdom advancement.

The **ongoing impact of the ascension** in our lives cannot be overstated. By ascending, Jesus did not just leave us with memories of His earthly ministry but with a living hope and a dynamic role in His heavenly kingdom. As believers seated with Him, our lives are to reflect the authority and victory He has given us. This means living out our faith with boldness, engaging in spiritual warfare with confidence, and transforming our environments with the power of the Gospel.

In sum, the ascension of Jesus encapsulates the **ultimate goal** of His mission—to bring us into a full realization of our identity and authority in Him. It's about moving beyond the cross to the throne, beyond redemption to reign. As we grasp this, we are transformed from followers into leaders, from believers into conquerors.

REFLECTIVE QUESTIONS

1. How does understanding the ascension of Christ change your perception of salvation?
2. In what ways do you see yourself seated with Christ in heavenly places impacting your daily life?
3. What aspects of your old life are you struggling to consider "dead" as Paul suggests we should?
4. How does the authority that Christ shares with us over death influence your understanding of spiritual warfare?
5. What steps can you take to more fully embrace your identity and authority in Christ as outlined in Ephesians?

ACTIONABLE STEPS

*   **Cultivate**: Cultivate a deeper understanding of your spiritual rebirth by regularly reflecting on scriptures related to Christ's death, burial, resurrection, and ascension. This meditation will reinforce your identity and authority in Him.
*   **Equip**: Equip yourself with knowledge of the ascension and its implications through Bible study and teachings. Understanding this can transform your spiritual life and how you engage with the world.
*   **Engage**: Engage in prayer and spiritual warfare with a new awareness of your seated position with Christ. Use this position to assert dominion over sin and spiritual darkness in your life and community.

Journaling Prompt

Reflect on what it means to be seated with Christ in heavenly places. How does this spiritual position affect your everyday decisions, interactions, and aspirations? Write about ways you can manifest this truth in your daily activities and relationships.

~

CHAPTER 2

THE DEVIL NEVER SAW IT COMING

Be encouraged that your understanding of the gospel is rooted in a unique and divine revelation that redefines power, authority, and victory in Christ. This revelation invites us into a life lived from a place of spiritual authority, seated with Christ in the heavenly realms, empowered to overcome the principalities of this world.

Ephesians 2:6 (NKJV): "and raised us up together, and made us sit together in the heavenly places in Christ Jesus,"

In this exploration of the profound truths Paul was divinely given, we uncover a narrative that revolutionizes our understanding of the gospel. The gospel I preach, much like Paul, is rooted not in teachings passed down by predecessors but in a direct **revelation from Jesus Christ**. This realization that the gospel came to Paul not through learned men but through Christ Himself emphasizes the **unique revelation** Paul received. It's this divine communication that shaped the very foundation of how we understand the work of Christ today.

Paul's past, marked by zeal for Jewish traditions, might seem at odds with his later mission. Yet, even as Saul, he was **predestined for a purpose** that would later manifest in his dramatic conversion on the road to Damascus. God's choice of Paul underscores a significant theme: God can transform anyone, regardless of their past, and use them for His divine purposes. This theme of transformation and purpose is a reminder that our past does not disqualify us from God's future plans.

The years Paul spent in Arabia and Damascus after his conversion were not times of idle retreat but crucial periods for deep reflection and preparation. These were **years of preparation** where Paul was secluded from the early Church's existing apostles, delving deep into the mysteries that had been revealed to him. This solitude was necessary for Paul to fully grasp and formulate the insights into Christ's work, insights that were not a reiteration of existing teachings but fresh revelations that would later challenge and extend the Church's understanding.

What stands out in Paul's writings is the insight that the mystery of Christ was so profound that it was hidden from everyone, including the spiritual principalities. This **hidden wisdom revealed** underscores the strategic brilliance of God's plan in Christ. It was a mystery so well concealed that even Satan himself was caught off guard by the crucifixion and resurrection of Jesus, events that Satan would have opposed had he understood their true significance. This revelation highlights the **mystery kept from Satan**, which was God's masterful play that turned what seemed like a victory for darkness into the ultimate defeat of evil and sin.

Furthermore, Paul reveals that Christ's work was not only about His own resurrection and ascension but was also about elevating humanity. Through Jesus, we were not only redeemed but also raised to sit with Him in heavenly places. This co-seating with Christ, which I refer to as **Christ's Ascension and**

Our Co-Seating, reveals the staggering breadth of Christ's victory—it was a victory shared with all who would believe in Him. This truth extends beyond traditional teachings and invites us into a dynamic and living reality where we are active participants in the divine.

Our **spiritual authority shared with believers** is a profound aspect of our faith that Paul was keen to communicate. This authority means that as believers, we are not just rescued souls but empowered sons and daughters of God, equipped to confront spiritual and earthly challenges with divine authority. This authority is not for a select few but for all who are in Christ, positioning us far above all principalities and powers.

Paul's mission went beyond personal salvation to include a corporate calling for the Church. He taught that the Church's role was to demonstrate the **wisdom of God** to the very principalities and powers that were once ignorant of God's plans. This role of the Church is critical, for it involves **revealing divine wisdom**, not just in words but through our very existence and the outworking of our faith in the world.

Lastly, the **commission to enforce and proclaim** the victory and authority of Christ is a mantle passed on to every believer. This commission challenges us to not only live in the light of this truth but to actively extend it through evangelism, teaching, and living out the principles of the Kingdom of God. This is our great commission—expansive and inclusive of the authority we've been given in Christ.

REFLECTIVE QUESTIONS

1. How does understanding Paul's unique reception of the gospel change your view of the New Testament scriptures?

2. In what ways do you see the period of isolation and preparation in your own spiritual journey reflecting Paul's time in Arabia and Damascus?
3. How does the concept of being 'co-seated' with Christ in heavenly places impact your understanding of your spiritual authority?
4. What are the implications of the revelation that Satan was unaware of God's full plan of salvation through Christ's work?
5. How can the Church today better fulfill its role in revealing God's wisdom to principalities and powers?

ACTIONABLE STEPS

- **Cultivate**: Cultivate a deeper personal understanding of the hidden truths of Christ's work by studying Paul's epistles with a focus on the revelations unique to him. Reflect on these insights in your personal prayer and study time.
- **Equip**: Equip yourself and others in your community with knowledge about our position in Christ through teaching and discipleship. Use resources that emphasize our identity and authority in Christ as revealed in the scriptures.
- **Engage**: Engage in spiritual warfare with a renewed understanding of your authority in Christ. Practical application includes intercessory prayer and declaring the truth of God's kingdom over your life, your family, and your community.

JOURNALING Prompt

Reflect on what it means to be seated with Christ in heavenly places beyond the initial salvation experience. Consider how this position affects your daily life and write about specific situations where you can apply this truth to exercise your authority in Christ.

$\sim$

CHAPTER 3
THE ASCENDED CHURCH

Be encouraged that through Christ's ascension, the Church has been given a position of unparalleled authority in both the spiritual and natural realms. This privilege is not just a reward but a responsibility to enforce Jesus' victory and reveal His Kingdom on earth as it is in heaven.

Ephesians 1:22-23 (NKJV): "And He put all things under His feet, and gave Him to be head over all things to the church, which is His body, the fullness of Him who fills all in all."

Why do I say that the ascension is what Satan fears the most? It is because of the **effect the ascension had in the realm of the spirit** over the kingdom of darkness. When Jesus ascended to the right hand of the Father, His victory over sin, death, and the devil was sealed, and the Church was elevated with Him to share in His authority. Jesus did not only redeem humanity but also destroyed the works of the devil, fulfilling 1 John 3:8. This act of redemption was both **redemptive for us and destructive for the devil**, demonstrating the complete defeat of darkness.

The roots of this battle go far deeper than mankind's existence. The **devil's sin from the beginning** was his prideful desire to be like God in power and authority, as described in Isaiah 14. This rebellion resulted in Lucifer's fall and the inception of his battle against God's Kingdom. After being cast out of heaven, Satan turned his attention to Adam, seeking to usurp the authority God had given to mankind. By leading Adam into sin, Satan gained temporary dominion, but his plans unraveled with the coming of Jesus.

Through His life, death, and resurrection, **Jesus regained the authority** that Adam lost, becoming the one Man with full dominion in heaven and on earth. The ascension and seating of Jesus at the right hand of the Father solidified this reality. It was not just a coronation of Christ but a demonstration to all spiritual realms of His absolute supremacy. Colossians 2:15 describes how Jesus disarmed principalities and powers, triumphing over them publicly in His ascension, leaving no doubt of His eternal authority.

Yet Jesus' ascension was not for Him alone. He intended to share this **position and authority with His body, the Church**, making us active participants in His victory. The Church is not just a gathering of believers on earth but a governing spiritual body in the heavenly places. We are seated with Christ, a position that reflects both privilege and responsibility. This **shared authority** enables us to represent Jesus not only in the physical realm but also in the spiritual, enforcing His victory over darkness.

Paul's prayer in Ephesians 1 underscores the necessity of **revelation to grasp these truths**. The ascension, our seating with Christ, and the authority we carry are not concepts the natural mind can fully comprehend. These are spiritual realities that must be received and believed by faith. The **heavenly places**, where we are seated with Christ, are the realms of spiritual activity and existence. Though invisible, they are real and dynamic, and our role in these realms is vital to the Church's mission.

The Church's assignment is twofold. We are called to represent Christ on earth and to operate as His governing body in the spirit realm. This **dual responsibility** ensures that His Kingdom is established and advanced both physically and spiritually. The ascension equips us for this mission, empowering the Church to overcome darkness and reveal the wisdom of God to all creation. Jesus declared that the gates of hell would not prevail against His Church, and this victory is realized when we fully embrace our role in both realms.

The ascension of Christ and our elevation with Him redefine what it means to be the Church. We are more than a community of believers; we are a spiritual force equipped to confront darkness and establish God's Kingdom. Now is the time for the Church to rise to this calling and occupy the position Christ has secured for us.

Reflective Questions

1. How does understanding the Church's shared authority with Christ change your perspective on your role in the Kingdom of God?
2. In what ways can you embrace the spiritual realities of being seated with Christ in heavenly places in your daily life?
3. How does Jesus' triumph over principalities and powers influence your confidence in spiritual warfare?

4. What does it mean for the Church to represent Christ in both the physical and spiritual realms?
5. How can you actively participate in the Church's mission to enforce Jesus' authority and advance His Kingdom?

ACTIONABLE STEPS

- **Cultivate**: Cultivate a deeper awareness of your spiritual position by meditating on scriptures that describe the ascension and our shared authority with Christ, such as Ephesians 1 and Colossians 2.
- **Equip**: Equip yourself with practical knowledge about spiritual warfare and the Church's role in the heavenly realms. Join or lead discussions in your community to explore these truths together.
- **Engage**: Engage in prayer and intercession with a focus on enforcing Christ's authority over darkness. Pray with boldness, declaring victory in areas where the enemy seeks to gain ground.

JOURNALING Prompt

Reflect on your role as part of the ascended Church. What specific situations in your life or community could benefit from the authority you have in Christ? Write about how you can actively engage in enforcing His victory both spiritually and practically.

CHAPTER 4
FILLING THE HEAVENS

Be encouraged that through Christ's ascension, the Church has been given a position of unparalleled authority in both the spiritual and natural realms. This privilege is not just a reward but a responsibility to enforce Jesus' victory and reveal His Kingdom on earth as it is in heaven.

Romans 8:17 (NKJV): "And if children, then heirs—heirs of God and joint heirs with Christ, if indeed we suffer with Him, that we may also be glorified together."

In revealing the impact of Christ's ascension, I am drawn deeply into the narrative of how the spiritual realm was altered, an event that marked the **devastation to the kingdom of darkness**. This was not a mere symbolic victory; it was a functional, decisive blow to Satan's operations, stripping him of the unchecked dominion he once wielded. This devastation was so complete that it redefined the spiritual landscape, ensuring that Satan could no longer operate without contest in the spirit realm.

Understanding the dynamics of authority through the biblical account of the Garden of Eden enriches our grasp of what exactly was restored through Christ. Initially, all authority on Earth was bestowed upon Adam, positioning him as the legal steward of the earthly realm. Satan, having been cast out of heaven, was forbidden to wield any such authority. However, through Adam's transgression, Satan manipulated humanity's fall, seizing the opportunity to operate under a stolen authority. This historical backdrop is crucial for appreciating the full scale of redemption—**Jesus' demonstrated authority** over spiritual and earthly domains showcased during His earthly ministry was not merely to awe the onlookers but to signify the restoration of dominion to mankind.

The **ascension's strategic impact** was a masterstroke in divine warfare. As Jesus ascended, He didn't just ascend in isolation but launched a decisive offensive into the spiritual territories, claiming back authority and displaying His supremacy for all to witness. By binding the strong man, as He described in His ministry, He was able to plunder Satan's house, reclaiming authority that was usurped. This was more than victory; it was a demonstration meant to be witnessed by all forces, angelic and demonic.

With this new reality, the role of the Church becomes profoundly evident. We, as the body of Christ, are not mere spectators but active participants in this ongoing spiritual saga. The Church's task is to continually enforce this victory, a role that extends beyond conventional understanding. The **fullness in the spiritual realm** that Christ intended involves the Church permeating every aspect of the spiritual realm, a strategy designed to leave no room for demonic resurgence. We are called to fill the heavens with the authority and presence of Christ, ensuring that no part of the spiritual or earthly realms remains under demonic influence.

The **assembling of the Church in spiritual realms** is not a metaphorical concept but a practical, necessary strategy for maintaining the victory Christ has secured. When we gather as believers, our assembly should be mirrored in the spiritual realm, where our collective authority can effectively counteract and displace demonic activities. This is where our spiritual battles are fought and won, not just in the physical gatherings but in our united spiritual presence in the heavenly places.

Moreover, the **displacement of satanic forces** is a task uniquely assigned to the Church. It is not enough to defend; we must actively reclaim and occupy spiritual territories. This proactive engagement in spiritual warfare ensures that the enemy's plans are thwarted and that God's Kingdom is manifest on Earth as it is in heaven.

The immense **authority of the Church** is both a privilege and a profound responsibility. We share in Christ's victory and are endowed with the authority to enforce it. This is not a passive inheritance but a call to active duty, where every believer is equipped to exercise dominion over darkness in the name of Jesus.

The **activation of the Church's authority** is critical. It is not enough to acknowledge our position in Christ; we must actively engage it. Every believer has a role to play in this divine orchestration, where our collective authority can influence outcomes in both the spiritual and natural realms.

REFLECTIVE QUESTIONS

1. How does understanding the Church's shared authority with Christ change your perspective on your role in the Kingdom of God?

2. In what ways can you more effectively 'fill' the spiritual realm with Christ's authority in your daily life?

3. What does it mean for you personally to participate in the displacement of satanic forces?

4. How can the Church better mobilize collectively to enforce Jesus' victory in the spiritual realms?

5. What are practical ways you can start exercising your spiritual authority in your community and beyond?

ACTIONABLE STEPS

- **Cultivate**: Develop a consistent spiritual discipline that includes prayer, fasting, and meditation on Scriptures related to authority and spiritual warfare. This will strengthen your spiritual foundation and prepare you for active engagement in the heavenly realms.

- **Equip**: Educate yourself and your community on the realities of spiritual warfare and the believer's authority in Christ. Organize study groups, workshops, or seminars to discuss and teach these principles extensively.

- **Engage**: Actively participate in strategic spiritual warfare through intercession, proclamation, and declaration. Target specific areas in your life, community, and the world where the enemy has held influence and declare Christ's rule and reign.

JOURNALING Prompt

Reflect on the areas of your life where you might have passively allowed satanic influences to operate. How can you begin to actively reclaim these areas for Christ? Write down specific steps you can take to assert your authority as a believer, based on the teachings of Christ's ascension and the role of the Church in spiritual warfare.

~

CHAPTER 5
Heaven and Heavenly Places

Be empowered by the knowledge that through Christ's ascension, you are elevated to participate in His authority. This grants you the divine mandate to enforce His victory over the spiritual darkness and manifest His kingdom here on Earth.

2 Peter 1:3 (NKJV): "His divine power has given to us all things that pertain to life and godliness, through the knowledge of Him who called us by glory and virtue."

Understanding the **distinction between 'Heaven' and 'heavenly places'** is crucial for every believer. Many confuse these terms, thinking they refer to the same experience, but they encapsulate two very different aspects of our spiritual journey and inheritance in Christ. While **Heaven is where we will ultimately reside** after our earthly journey, enjoying eternal rest and freedom from sin, 'heavenly places' refer to a spiritual realm where we are called to actively engage now. It is in these **heavenly places** that we exercise the authority granted to us through Christ's victory over sin and death. This authority is not just theoretical; it's a practical, actionable mandate to influence both the spiritual and physical realms.

The **role of heavenly places in spiritual warfare** is profound. Unlike Heaven, where peace and worship prevail without opposition, heavenly places are battlegrounds. Here, believers are equipped and expected to contend with spiritual forces opposing God's kingdom. It's where the church's authority to bind and loose is most needed and most effective, aimed directly at disrupting the schemes of darkness and advancing God's kingdom on Earth. As believers, understanding this realm's reality is essential for living out our faith effectively.

This authority we discuss isn't just for a future time; it has immediate implications and applications. The common misconception that we must wait until Heaven to experience any benefits of our faith diminishes the powerful truth that **benefits exist now and to come**. Paul's teachings make it clear that while we look forward to the fullness of our redemption in Heaven, there is much to be grasped and utilized in the here and now. The spiritual blessings and authority we have in Christ are not on pause until we pass from this world.

When we first believed in Christ, we were **sealed with the Holy Spirit, who is the earnest of our inheritance**. This sealing is not just a mark of ownership but an empowerment, equipping us with a foretaste of Heaven while we operate on Earth. This concept of the 'earnest'—like a down payment—ensures that while our ultimate redemption will be realized in Heaven, there is a substantial, real experience of God's kingdom and power available to us right here and right now.

Our **spiritual authority in action** can be vividly seen in how Jesus dealt with the demonic, sickness, and nature. His life was a demonstration of the kingdom of God breaking into the human realm, a preview of what He expects us to continue. By understanding and exercising our authority in Christ, we are following in the footsteps of Jesus, bringing healing, deliverance, and Kingdom order wherever we go.

REFLECTIVE QUESTIONS

1. How does understanding the distinction between Heaven and heavenly places change your perception of spiritual authority?
2. What are some ways you can more actively engage in spiritual warfare using the authority you have in Christ?
3. How does the Holy Spirit's role as the earnest of our inheritance impact your daily walk with God?
4. In what practical ways can you start to manifest aspects of Heaven in your current environment?
5. What steps can you take to prepare both spiritually and practically for your eternal reality in Heaven while living victoriously on earth?

ACTIONABLE STEPS

- **Cultivate**: Develop a daily prayer strategy that focuses on utilizing your spiritual authority to bring heavenly realities into your earthly circumstances. This includes intercessory prayer and declarations based on scriptural promises.
- **Equip**: Equip yourself and your community with knowledge and understanding of spiritual realms and authority through Bible study and teachings on

spiritual warfare. Understanding your position in Christ is crucial for effective engagement.

- **Engage**: Regularly engage in community outreach and ministry activities that reflect the kingdom of Heaven on earth. This includes healing ministries, deliverance, and preaching the Gospel with the authority Christ has given you.

JOURNALING **Prompt**

Reflect on your current understanding and exercise of spiritual authority. How can you more effectively use this authority to impact your community and beyond? Write about specific situations where you can apply your heavenly mandate to bring change and alignment with God's kingdom.

CHAPTER 6

CROWNED BY GRACE

Be empowered by the truth that your heavenly seating is by grace, giving you a majestic authority shared with Christ.

Hebrews 1:3 (NKJV): "Who being the brightness of His glory and the express image of His person, and upholding all things by the word of His power, when He had by Himself purged our sins, sat down at the right hand of the Majesty on high."

As we delve into the majestic realm where Christ resides, we recognize that the **right hand of the Father** is not merely a position of authority but a place resonating with divine majesty. This majesty, or **megalosyne** in Greek, conveys grandeur on a scale that is both splendid and overwhelming, denoting a rank of greatness that belongs solely to Christ. Understanding this helps us appreciate the unique position that Christ holds—He alone is appointed to sit at this place of honor, a seat reserved for the One who upholds all things by the word of His power, having purified our sins and triumphed gloriously.

This majestic position that Christ occupies is not just a symbol of His victory but a tangible reflection of His authority, which far exceeds that of the angels. This hierarchy in the spiritual realm indicates that Christ, by inheritance, has obtained a name more excellent than any other. It is from this understanding of Christ's supreme authority and majesty that we, as believers, draw our confidence to engage the world and the spiritual forces that contend against the Kingdom of God.

Our journey as believers mirrors that of Christ's—from suffering on the cross to reigning in glory. We are no longer mere sinners; through the cross, we have been transformed into **royal and majestic sons and daughters**, called to reflect the glory of Him who has called us out of darkness. This transformation is not merely symbolic but represents a profound change in our spiritual identity and standing. As a **royal priesthood and a holy nation**, we have been given the authority to act on behalf of the Kingdom of Heaven, showcasing the praises of God through our lives and actions.

This identity as God's chosen people underscores our role as His representatives on earth. Just as earthly royalty bear the responsibility of upholding the dignity of their nations, we are tasked with living out the virtues of the Kingdom of God, demonstrating His justice, mercy, and love in every interaction. This understanding compels us to live not as citizens of this world but as ambassadors of an eternal kingdom.

Moreover, the notion that we are **God's inheritance**, as revealed through scripture, emphasizes the reciprocal nature of our relationship with the Divine. Just as we inherit eternal life and a new identity in Christ, God views us as His cherished possession, a people set apart to reflect His glory. This mutual inheritance is a profound mystery and a powerful motivator that should inspire us to live lives worthy of our calling.

The full realization of our identity involves an **identity shift** that many find challenging. To see oneself as a part of God's royal lineage requires a mental and spiritual shift—a transformation in how we view ourselves and our purpose in the world. This shift is not optional but essential for those who wish to fully embrace their destiny in Christ.

In living out this identity, it is crucial to recognize that everything we are and everything we have achieved in the spiritual realm is by grace. **Grace is the basis of our position** at the right hand of the Father, alongside Christ. This grace is not a passive concept but an active force that enables us to overcome the world, not by our strength but through the power of the Holy Spirit who seals and empowers us.

As we engage in **spiritual warfare**, knowing our position in Christ gives us the confidence to stand firm against the forces of darkness. We do not fight for victory; we fight from a place of victory, one already won by Christ. Our role is to enforce and manifest that victory in our lives and our world, continually advancing the boundaries of His Kingdom.

Living out our royal calling involves more than understanding our position; it requires actively **walking in authority**, exercising the dominion that Christ has shared with us. This means taking every opportunity to manifest the Kingdom of God in our lives, whether through prayer, worship, service, or spiritual warfare.

As we continue to explore what it means to be **crowned by grace**, let us strive to live lives that not only reflect Christ's victory but also extend His reign in every corner of our influence. Let our lives be a testament to the power and grace of God, who has called us to share in His eternal glory.

· · ·

REFLECTIVE QUESTIONS

1. How does understanding your position as a royal heir influence your daily decisions and interactions?
2. In what ways can you more actively engage in spiritual warfare using the authority you have in Christ?
3. How does the Holy Spirit's role as the earnest of our inheritance impact your daily walk with God?
4. In what practical ways can you start to manifest aspects of Heaven in your current environment?
5. What steps can you take to prepare both spiritually and practically for your eternal reality in Heaven while living victoriously on earth?

ACTIONABLE STEPS

- **Cultivate**: Develop a daily awareness of your royal identity through meditation on scriptures about our position in Christ. Let this truth profoundly influence how you view yourself and the world around you.
- **Equip**: Enhance your understanding of spiritual warfare by studying biblical texts that outline our authority and the armor of God. Equip yourself for daily battles by dressing in spiritual armor.
- **Engage**: Take proactive steps to manifest the kingdom of God in your surroundings. Engage in community outreach, intercessory prayer, and other kingdom-building activities that demonstrate the power and love of Christ to others.

. . .

JOURNALING Prompt

Reflect on the reality of your heavenly seating and authority. Journal about how this truth can transform your approach to challenges and opportunities. Consider specific areas in your life where you need to assert your authority more confidently and ask God to help you live out your heavenly mandate more fully.

CHAPTER 7
SPIRITUAL BLESSINGS

Embrace the full measure of your inheritance in Christ, recognizing that spiritual blessings empower you to manifest God's kingdom on earth as it is in heaven.

"But God, who is rich in mercy, because of His great love with which He loved us, even when we were dead in trespasses, made us alive together with Christ (by grace you have been saved), and raised us up together, and made us sit together in the heavenly places in Christ Jesus" (Ephesians 2:4-6 NKJV).

In my reflections and teachings, I've emphasized that while **spiritual over material blessings** are often overshadowed by the latter, their significance cannot be overstated. The true wealth of a believer lies not in earthly riches but in the profound **spiritual blessings** that we have been granted through Christ. These blessings, detailed in Ephesians, serve not only as markers of God's favor but as functional tools that empower us to operate effectively in the spiritual realm.

These blessings are not arbitrary; they are **authorizations and access** granted to us, allowing us to wield the privileges once reserved for Christ alone. This access transforms how we engage with the world and the spirit realm, affirming our place as children of God chosen before the foundation of the world. Our **inheritance and rights**, as detailed by Paul, are not future promises but current realities, available and accessible right now.

Each believer is **sealed by the Spirit**, a mark of divine ownership and protection, which also activates our spiritual blessings. This sealing is not just a mark; it's a guarantee, a deposit confirming that what God has promised He will indeed deliver. Through this, we carry the assurance of our salvation and the weight of our inheritance, which includes more than eternal life; it encompasses a life of power and authority here on earth.

Yet, the challenge many face is fully embracing these truths. We must undergo an **identity shift** from seeing ourselves as mere mortals to recognizing our royal lineage as kings and priests in God's kingdom. This shift isn't merely about confidence; it's about realizing the operational shift in how we pray, worship, and engage with both the physical and spiritual realms.

By understanding that these blessings are part of our **empowerment for dominion**, we can begin to exercise authority over the powers of darkness that we are told we will trample upon. This dominion is not for our glorification but for the manifestation of God's kingdom on earth as it is in heaven. We are called to **live like heirs**, fully embracing the rights and responsibilities that come with our spiritual lineage.

To activate these blessings, we must believe in their reality and step into them with faith. The spiritual realm operates differently from the natural; it requires faith and spiritual insight to navigate and utilize the blessings therein. **Activation of bless-**

ings involves more than acknowledgment; it demands engagement and application.

In essence, my dear reader, as we delve deeper into understanding these truths, let us move beyond mere acknowledgment into a profound engagement with our spiritual inheritance. Let us live not as beggars at the gate of the kingdom but as sons and daughters within it, fully equipped and **empowered to manifest the kingdom of God** here and now.

As we reflect on these truths, consider how they can transform your approach to life and ministry. Are you walking in the fullness of your spiritual blessings? Are you fully utilizing the access and authority granted to you? These are not just theological concepts but practical realities meant to influence how we live daily.

To further explore and apply these revelations, consider how you can cultivate a deeper relationship with the Holy Spirit, equip yourself with knowledge of your spiritual rights, and engage in activities that manifest God's power and love in the world around you. As we do so, we live out the reality of our heavenly citizenship here on earth, fully enjoying the spiritual blessings that are ours in Christ Jesus.

REFLECTIVE QUESTIONS

1. How does understanding your spiritual blessings change the way you view your daily challenges and opportunities?

2. In what ways can you more actively engage with the Holy Spirit to unlock deeper revelations of your spiritual inheritance?

3. How does the concept of being sealed by the Spirit influence your sense of identity and purpose?

4. What practical steps can you take to manifest your spiritual blessings in your community or ministry?
5. How can you cultivate a lifestyle that consistently reflects the authority and power you have in Christ?

ACTIONABLE STEPS

- **Cultivate** a daily practice of prayer and meditation on Scriptures related to your spiritual blessings to deepen your connection with God.
- **Equip** yourself with knowledge about your spiritual authority through Bible study and teachings from trusted spiritual leaders.
- **Engage** in community service or ministry activities that allow you to exercise your spiritual gifts and callings.

JOURNALING Prompt

Reflect on a situation where you felt powerless or defeated. How can you apply your understanding of spiritual blessings and authority to change the outcome if a similar situation arises in the future?

~

CHAPTER 8

SPIRITUALLY ASCENDING

God's desire is for us to live in the reality of His heavenly authority while we are still here on earth. Jesus demonstrated this life by living in the Spirit, connected to the Father, and walking in victory over natural limitations. We are invited into the same ascended life, where our thoughts, words, and actions align with heaven's purposes. This is not beyond our reach, for the Holy Spirit empowers us to live in this reality daily. Let us embrace this calling with renewed minds and hearts filled with His presence.

"If then you were raised with Christ, seek those things which are above, where Christ is, sitting at the right hand of God." Colossians 3:1 NKJV

Living the ascended life is an invitation into the supernatural dimension of walking with God, something Jesus demonstrated throughout His earthly ministry. **Spiritual ascension is not about mystical escapades but about living daily with a heavenly mindset.** Jesus operated

47

from heavenly places while living in the earth realm, revealing that it is possible to function in the Spirit and carry out God's will here and now. **He showed us the power of the Holy Spirit, who enables us to overcome natural limitations and access spiritual authority.** This is the same Spirit who fills us today, empowering us to fulfill our assignments just as Jesus fulfilled His.

Understanding the difference between Jesus's ministry and mission is crucial. His ministry was to seek and save the lost, while His mission was to build His Church and establish the Kingdom of Heaven on earth. The authority to bind and loose, as Jesus described, is not merely symbolic but practical—it is the language of ascension. **When we live in alignment with this authority, we begin to function as Christ intended, carrying forward His mission on earth.**

To do this, we must embrace the transformative power of repentance. **Repentance, as Jesus taught, is not only about turning from sin but about adopting a completely new way of thinking—one aligned with the Kingdom of Heaven.** Without this renewed mindset, we cannot fully access the spiritual authority God has given us. God's ways are higher than ours, and repentance allows us to step into His higher thoughts and purposes.

Our identity as seated with Christ in heavenly places is the foundation of spiritual ascension. This position is not earned but is a gift of grace, secured by Jesus's finished work. The enemy may try to convince us otherwise, but our authority is rooted in Christ, not in our own merit. By embracing this truth, we can walk confidently in the Spirit, knowing we operate from a position of victory.

One of the greatest hindrances to living the ascended life is an unrenewed mind. While our spirits are already seated with Christ, our minds must catch up to this reality. Without a renewed mind, we will continue to act as though we are unseated. This is why Jesus continually emphasized the need to repent and align our thinking with the Kingdom. Renewing our minds is not optional; it is essential for living in the fullness of our spiritual authority.

Jesus's example shows us the power of living in alignment with the Father's will. He only did what He saw the Father doing and said what He heard the Father saying. Through the Holy Spirit, we have access to the same guidance, enabling us to live with heavenly authority in every aspect of our lives. **Worshiping in spirit and truth is another key to the ascended life.** True worship is not confined to physical locations or rituals; it is about connecting with God in the Spirit and aligning our lives with His will.

Finally, **the ascended life requires intentionality.** We must consciously choose to think, speak, and act from our heavenly position. This is not automatic but requires daily effort to renew our minds and align with the Spirit's leading. The more we walk in this reality, the more we will see God's power manifest in and through us.

This is the life Jesus died to give us—a life of spiritual authority, supernatural power, and intimate connection with the Father. Let us not waste this incredible gift but embrace the ascended life and walk in the fullness of all that Christ has secured for us.

REFLECTIVE QUESTIONS

1. How does understanding Jesus's dual purpose of ministry and mission inspire you to live with greater intentionality?

2. In what ways can you align your daily thoughts and actions with your spiritual position in Christ?
3. What steps can you take to embrace repentance as a change of thinking rather than just turning from sin?
4. How can you rely on the Holy Spirit's guidance to live more fully in your heavenly authority?
5. What practical changes can you make to live with a renewed mind and embrace the ascended life?

ACTIONABLE STEPS

- **Cultivate** a Kingdom mindset by daily meditating on scriptures that affirm your position in Christ.
- **Equip** yourself with the knowledge of the Holy Spirit's role in empowering your spiritual authority.
- **Engage** in intentional worship and prayer, focusing on aligning your thoughts and actions with God's will.

JOURNALING **Prompt**

Reflect on a recent experience where you felt disconnected from your spiritual authority. Write about what steps you can take to renew your mind and align with the ascended life Christ has given you.

CHAPTER 9

I GO TO PREPARE A PLACE FOR YOU

Let your heart rest in the assurance of Jesus's words. The place He has prepared for us is not simply a future heavenly home but a spiritual reality we can access even now. In this dwelling, we find comfort, authority, and the abiding presence of the Holy Spirit, guiding us into all truth. We are no longer orphans; we are children of the Father, living from a prepared place of eternal connection with Him.

"In My Father's house are many mansions; if it were not so, I would have told you. I go to prepare a place for you." John 14:2 NKJV

Understanding Jesus's promise that He would "prepare a place for you" requires seeing it as more than just a future reality in Heaven. **Jesus referred to a spiritual dwelling place, an intimate connection with the Father accessible even while we live on earth.** This prepared place is established in the spiritual realm, where we are seated with

Christ in heavenly places. **Through the Holy Spirit, Jesus has given us the capacity to function in this divine reality.**

The disciples struggled to understand what Jesus meant, asking Him where He was going and how they could follow. **Jesus clarified that He is the way, the truth, and the life, emphasizing that access to the Father is through Him alone.** This understanding is foundational for living in the reality of the ascension. As believers, we enter this prepared place through faith in Jesus, where our spiritual inheritance is made manifest.

The promise of the Holy Spirit is key to this spiritual dwelling. Jesus explained that after His departure, the Spirit of truth would come to teach and guide us. The Holy Spirit is not just a comforter but an enabler, giving us the ability to live as Jesus did, performing greater works and glorifying the Father. **This indwelling of the Spirit signifies the transition from Jesus being with us to being in us.**

The prepared place is not only about Heaven; it is also about living in God's presence here and now. **Jesus's reference to mansions or abiding places speaks of our position in the Father's house—permanently connected to Him, enjoying the privileges of being His children.** This understanding empowers us to live with authority, asking in Jesus's name and receiving from the Father.

Our inheritance in Christ has two installments: the down payment we experience now and the fullness we will receive in eternity. Paul's writings in Philippians remind us that while to be with Christ in Heaven is "far better," there is profound purpose and blessing in our current lives. We are called to live from our spiritual position, embracing the reality of our inheritance now.

The works that Jesus did—and greater works—are possible because of this spiritual position. **From this prepared place, we engage in the Father's mission, praying in Jesus's name and**

receiving what we ask. This is not just a promise for the future but a reality for today. Living in this truth, we glorify the Father through the Son, fulfilling the mission of the Kingdom on earth.

Finally, **Jesus's words remind us that we are not orphans.** His ascension and the sending of the Holy Spirit ensure that we are never alone. This abiding presence transforms our lives, enabling us to live in constant fellowship with the Father. Jesus's preparation of this place for us is the ultimate expression of His love and commitment, inviting us to dwell with Him now and forever.

REFLECTIVE QUESTIONS

1. How does understanding Jesus's prepared place as a current reality change your perspective on your relationship with the Father?
2. What does it mean to you that the Holy Spirit enables you to live as Jesus lived, performing greater works?
3. In what ways can you embrace the reality of your spiritual inheritance today while anticipating its fullness in eternity?
4. How does knowing you are permanently connected to the Father empower you to pray with boldness and faith?
5. What steps can you take to live more intentionally from your position in the heavenly places?

ACTIONABLE STEPS

- **Cultivate** your awareness of the Holy Spirit's presence by daily seeking His guidance in prayer and worship.
- **Equip** yourself with scriptures that affirm your spiritual position in Christ, meditating on them to renew your mind.
- **Engage** in acts of faith that reflect your heavenly authority, such as praying boldly for others and speaking life into situations.

JOURNALING Prompt

Reflect on what it means to you that Jesus has prepared a place for you in the Father's house. Write about how you can live from this spiritual position in your daily life, walking in the authority and peace that come from being seated with Christ.

CHAPTER 10

ANGELS ASCENDING AND DESCENDING

The ascension of Jesus shifted the entire structure of spiritual authority, placing the Church in a position of governing supremacy in the heavenly places. This divine elevation empowers us to operate as vessels of God's will on earth, with angelic beings responding to our prayers and words of faith. As heirs of salvation, we now carry a responsibility to release God's activity into the earth realm, bringing His kingdom purposes to fruition.

"Are they not all ministering spirits sent forth to minister for those who will inherit salvation?" Hebrews 1:14 NKJV

The ascension of Jesus granted the Church an extraordinary role in the spirit realm. **When Christ ascended, He transferred spiritual authority to us, enabling the Church to operate in dominion over the heavenly places.** This supremacy is not just about defeating the powers of darkness but also about releasing God's divine plans and purposes into the earth.

Angels are integral to this process. They are not only witnesses to God's mysteries but also active participants in the fulfillment of His will. Peter wrote that even angels longed to understand the unfolding plan of salvation, a mystery that became clearer with the revelation of the new creation seated with Christ. Now, angels minister to us as heirs of salvation, just as they ministered to Jesus during His earthly ministry.

Jesus's interaction with Nathanael, as recorded in John 1:44-51, reveals a profound ascension reality. **He described a life under an open heaven, where angels ascend and descend upon the Son of Man.** This imagery reflects continuous spiritual activity between Heaven and earth, orchestrated by Jesus and now extended to us through Him.

The vision of Jacob's ladder in Genesis 28 serves as a prophetic picture of Jesus. Jacob's dream of a ladder connecting Heaven and earth symbolized Christ as the gateway between the two realms. When Jesus came, He embodied Bethel —the house of God—and opened a spiritual portal for Heaven's activity to flow into the earth through His life and ministry.

Angels are not just observers; they are active participants in God's kingdom. They accompanied Jesus at His birth, ministered to Him during His earthly trials, and were ready to intervene at His command. Jesus's authority over the angelic realm was demonstrated when He declared that He could summon legions of angels if needed. This same authority has now been extended to us as co-heirs with Christ.

Hebrews 1:14 clarifies the role of angels in relation to believers. They are ministering spirits sent to serve those who will inherit salvation. This profound truth means that angels are actively working in our lives, responding to our prayers, declarations, and faith. They ascend and descend, carrying out God's purposes as we align ourselves with His will.

Living under an open heaven means we are the ladders

through which angels move. **Our words, prayers, and actions create spiritual activity that impacts both Heaven and earth.** This is a great privilege and responsibility, requiring us to walk in faith, speak God's Word, and remain in alignment with His Spirit.

The ascension of Jesus ensures that angelic assistance is part of our spiritual inheritance. Whether we see them or not, angels are constantly at work, advancing God's kingdom and protecting His children. As we embrace this reality, we can live with greater confidence, knowing that we are never alone in our spiritual journey.

REFLECTIVE QUESTIONS

1. How does understanding the role of angels as ministering spirits change the way you pray and live?
2. What does it mean to you that Jesus opened a portal between Heaven and earth, allowing continuous spiritual activity?
3. In what ways can you align your words and actions to activate angelic assistance in your life?
4. How can the imagery of Jacob's ladder inspire your faith in God's connection between Heaven and earth?
5. What steps can you take to live more consciously under an open heaven, embracing your spiritual authority?

ACTIONABLE STEPS

- **Cultivate** a lifestyle of speaking God's Word, knowing that angels respond to His commands through your faith-filled declarations.
- **Equip** yourself with scriptures that affirm your authority in Christ and the role of angels, meditating on them regularly to strengthen your understanding.
- **Engage** in acts of obedience that align with God's will, creating opportunities for angelic activity to manifest in your life and ministry.

JOURNALING Prompt

Reflect on the reality of angels ascending and descending in response to your prayers and words. Write about how you can live more intentionally, embracing your role in releasing God's activity into the earth through faith and spiritual alignment.

THE FINISHED WORK

You and I have entered into the finished work of Christ! All of the works of redemption have been completed. The victory has already been won, and we are now seated in heavenly places with Christ. Everything we need—our healing, deliverance, provision, and salvation—has been secured through His sacrifice. Our responsibility is to live from this position of victory, enforcing the authority He has granted us. Let this truth transform how you think, speak, and act, as you embrace the reality of His completed work on your behalf.

"For by one offering He has perfected forever those who are being sanctified." Hebrews 10:14 (NKJV)

The finished work of Christ is the foundation of our faith and victory. **Every work of redemption was completed when Jesus declared, "It is finished."** His ascension and seating at the right hand of the Father signify not only His authority but also ours as co-heirs with Him. **We are called to enforce the victory that Christ has already won,**

standing firm against the enemy who is already defeated. Our prayers and declarations carry the authority of heaven, and we are empowered to operate from this seated position in every area of life.

God's promises are fulfilled entirely in Christ, as He is the Seed through which all nations are blessed. This truth shifts our perspective from striving to receive to resting in the fact that the promises are already ours. **Through Christ, we inherit every blessing and promise, living in the abundance He has secured.** Our position in Him means we are equipped to live victoriously, overcoming every challenge with the confidence that we operate in His finished work.

This finished work also unites us as one body. **In Christ, there is no division based on race, gender, or status.** We are all heirs according to the promise, sharing equally in the inheritance of His Kingdom. This revelation reminds us that God's justice and equality are already implemented in His Kingdom. **Our citizenship in heaven calls us to live by Kingdom principles, reflecting the righteousness and unity of God's rule.**

Living in the finished work requires a renewed mind. **We must see ourselves as joint heirs with Christ, seated in heavenly places, and empowered to live as overcomers.** This understanding transforms our faith from hesitant hope to bold confidence. Our words, actions, and prayers align with the truth of our identity in Him, bringing the reality of heaven into our daily lives. **Every blessing, healing, and victory has already been secured, and our faith activates their manifestation in our lives.**

REFLECTIVE QUESTIONS

1. What does it mean for you personally to live in the finished work of Christ?
2. How can you shift your prayers and mindset to align with the truth that God's promises are already fulfilled in Christ?
3. What areas of your life still feel like a struggle, and how can you apply the reality of being seated with Christ to those situations?
4. How does the unity found in Christ challenge the divisions and inequalities in the world?
5. In what ways can you daily remind yourself of your identity as a joint heir with Christ?

ACTIONABLE STEPS

- **Cultivate** your understanding of the finished work by meditating on scriptures that affirm your position in Christ.
- **Equip** yourself with the Word of God to enforce your authority over the enemy, speaking truth and life into your circumstances.
- **Engage** with others by sharing the transformative power of living in Christ's completed work, encouraging them to embrace their inheritance.

Journaling **Prompt**

Write about an area of your life where you need to fully embrace the finished work of Christ. Reflect on the promises of God that apply to that situation and how you can live from a position of victory, not striving.

CHAPTER 12
UNMOVABLE SEAT

You and I have been seated in an unmovable position in heavenly places with Christ Jesus. This seat of authority is far above all principalities and powers, and it is secured not by our actions, but by what Jesus accomplished on the cross and through His resurrection. His intercession ensures that we remain reconciled with God, no matter the challenges we face. This revelation changes everything about how we live, pray, and confront the enemy. It calls us to walk boldly in the authority that has been given to us as heirs with Christ.

"Therefore, my beloved brethren, be steadfast, immovable, always abounding in the work of the Lord, knowing that your labor is not in vain in the Lord." 1 Corinthians 15:58 (NKJV)

The **unmovable seat we occupy in Christ** is a gift of grace. **Jesus intercedes for us continuously, ensuring our reconciliation with the Father** and guaranteeing that nothing can unseat us. This position of authority is not earned by works but is granted through His finished work. **We have been invited to sit with Him in heavenly places, a seat that is permanent and secure.** This means that our spiritual authority does not fluctuate based on our emotions or failures; it is steadfast because it is grounded in Christ's accomplishments.

Understanding this seat gives us a new perspective on spiritual warfare. **The enemy cannot unseat us, but he will try to deceive us into thinking otherwise.** Our job is to enforce the victory already won, using the authority of the Word of God and the power of prayer. **When we understand our seated position, we operate from victory, not for victory.** This is why the revelation of the ascension is so critical—it reminds us of the authority we carry as those who are seated with Christ.

Living from this unmovable seat requires faith and a deep assurance of who we are in Christ. As Paul prayed for the Ephesians, we must pray for our eyes to be opened to the hope of our calling and the riches of our inheritance in Him. **This position calls us to live in alignment with the Kingdom of God, exercising our authority with confidence and humility.** Even when we face opposition or resistance, we remain steadfast, knowing that Jesus has already triumphed over every power of darkness.

The **ascension also reveals Jesus as our eternal Intercessor,** who stands between us and the Father, ensuring our peace with God. This role of intercession is not about continual pleading but about a fixed and eternal position of advocacy. **Because He lives forever to make intercession for us, we remain in right standing with God, even in our moments of weakness or failure.** This truth brings freedom from fear and a boldness to live out our faith with confidence.

Our position in Christ calls us to a life of consecration and preparedness. **When the enemy resists, we must respond**

from a place of faith, not fear. Living a life of prayer and devotion keeps our faith strong and ensures that we are ready to confront any challenge with the authority of Christ. **The key to victory is remaining steadfast, grounded in the truth of our unmovable seat.** This is the position from which we confront every lie, every attack, and every attempt of the enemy to derail us.

REFLECTIVE QUESTIONS

1. How does the revelation of being seated in heavenly places change how you view spiritual warfare?
2. What steps can you take to deepen your understanding of the authority you have in Christ?
3. In what areas of your life do you struggle to believe in the permanence of your position in Christ?
4. How can the knowledge of Jesus's intercession for you bring greater confidence in your relationship with God?
5. What practical ways can you remind yourself daily of the unmovable seat you occupy in Christ?

ACTIONABLE STEPS

- **Cultivate** a habit of meditating on scriptures that affirm your seated position in Christ, such as Ephesians 2:6 and Romans 8:34.
- **Equip** yourself by living a life of prayer and fasting to keep your faith strong and ready for any spiritual resistance.

- **Engage** with others by sharing the truth of their unmovable seat in Christ, encouraging them to live boldly in their authority.

Journaling **Prompt**

Reflect on a time when you felt spiritually defeated. How does the truth of your unmovable seat in Christ change how you view that experience? Write about how you can apply this revelation to future challenges.

CHAPTER 13
ASCENSION LIVING

The ascended life is not something we must strive to attain; it is a reality that has been gifted to us through Christ. This life is not marked by the absence of challenges but by a profound peace, joy, and authority that enable us to rise above them. We are not called to merely survive but to thrive, reflecting the light and love of Jesus in a world longing for hope. Let this be the day you fully embrace your position in Him, walking in the abundant life He has secured for you.

"Peace I leave with you, My peace I give to you; not as the world gives do I give to you. Let not your heart be troubled, neither let it be afraid." John 14:27 NKJV

As I reflect on the life of Jesus, I see a perfect example of what it means to live an ascended life. **Jesus came to earth not because He needed salvation or a position with the Father but to secure that position for us.** His entire mission was to pave the way for us to be seated at the right hand of God, demonstrating what the ascended life looks like, even before the cross. From His teachings to His actions, Jesus modeled a life of authority, love, peace, and joy, showing us the life we are called to live.

The ascended life is a life rooted in authority and abundance. Jesus, though functioning as a man, operated with the authority of heaven, displaying the power and privilege available to us. He spoke about abundant life, using the Greek word "zoe," which signifies the God-kind of life—a life of divine quality and fullness. This abundant life is not something we wait for in eternity. It is a life we can experience here and now, a life superior to anything the natural world offers. **Through His teachings, Jesus revealed that the ascended life begins with a transformation of our thinking and living.** He called His followers to think differently, to embrace love and peace, and to reflect the values of the Kingdom in every area of their lives.

One of the first lessons Jesus taught was the necessity of internal transformation. **Without a change in our hearts and minds, the ascended life cannot manifest outwardly.** In His Sermon on the Mount, Jesus blessed those who exhibited qualities such as meekness, mercy, and purity of heart, showing that the ascended life requires a commitment to living in love, peace, and humility. This is not just about doing extraordinary miracles but about embodying the fruits of the Spirit in our daily lives. **Love, especially, is foundational to ascension living.** Jesus commanded us to love one another, even our enemies, because love is the hallmark of a life aligned with God.

Peace is another cornerstone of the ascended life, and Jesus demonstrated this beautifully. When He calmed the storm, His peace was so unshakable that He could sleep through the chaos. He left us this same peace, a divine peace that surpasses all understanding. When we operate from this peace, we can face life's challenges without fear, knowing that we are anchored in Christ. **This peace allows us to confront spiritual battles with authority, knowing that we are seated far above principalities and powers.** It empowers us to speak to our circumstances with faith and confidence.

Living the ascended life also means walking in joy. **Jesus promised that His joy would remain in us, a joy that is complete and overflowing.** This joy is not dependent on external circumstances but is rooted in our relationship with God. It is a joy that shines brightly, drawing others to the hope we have in Christ. **As we live in love, joy, and peace, we become a light to the world, reflecting the glory of the ascended life.**

The ascended life is not just about the power we wield but also about the humility we display. Jesus, though exalted, humbled Himself and became a servant. He lived a life of complete obedience to the Father, demonstrating that true greatness in the Kingdom comes through servanthood. As we follow His example, we find that humility opens the door to greater blessings and deeper intimacy with God.

Finally, living the ascended life is a call to represent the Kingdom of God on earth. **We are not just beneficiaries of this abundant life but ambassadors of it.** Our lives should reflect the superior quality of life found in Christ, inspiring others to seek the hope and transformation we have experienced. **This is not just about attending church services but about living a life of service and love that impacts families, communities, and nations.**

My prayer for you is that you embrace the ascended life in its fullness. Let love, peace, and joy become the hallmarks of your daily walk. Recognize the authority you have in Christ and use it to bring hope and healing to those around you. May your life be a testimony of God's abundant grace and a beacon of light in a world longing for truth and love.

REFLECTIVE QUESTIONS

1. How does understanding the ascended life change your perspective on your daily challenges?
2. In what ways can you cultivate love, peace, and joy in your interactions with others?
3. How does Jesus' example inspire you to live with humility and servanthood?
4. What steps can you take to align your thoughts and actions with the values of the Kingdom?
5. How can you become a light in your community, reflecting the ascended life to those around you?

ACTIONABLE STEPS

- **Cultivate**: Begin each day by meditating on God's Word and His promises for the abundant life, letting them shape your thoughts and actions.
- **Equip**: Practice speaking peace and joy into your circumstances, drawing on the authority and power you have in Christ.
- **Engage**: Be intentional about showing love and kindness in your relationships, reflecting the character of Christ in all you do.

JOURNALING Prompt

Reflect on an area of your life where you struggle to live out the ascended life. Write about the steps you can take to align with God's peace, love, and authority in that area, and commit to embracing the abundant life He has promised.

CHAPTER 14
ASCENSION POWER

The power of the ascension is not reserved for a select few; it is an inheritance for all believers. Jesus declared that the works He did, we would also do, and even greater works, because He ascended and seated us with Him. This truth calls us to a life of faith and authority. We are equipped and empowered by the Spirit to walk in victory and demonstrate the Kingdom of God in every area of our lives. Do not let fear or doubt hold you back from stepping into this divine reality.

"But you shall receive power when the Holy Spirit has come upon you; and you shall be witnesses to Me in Jerusalem, and in all Judea and Samaria, and to the end of the earth." Acts 1:8 NKJV

The life Jesus lived on earth was not only a demonstration of God's love and authority but a preview of the **ascension power** available to us. When Jesus promised that we would do greater works, He wasn't exaggerating. This was His way of preparing us for the spiritual authority we would receive through His ascension. **Our position in Christ means we are seated far above all principalities and powers,** granting us access to the same authority Jesus operated in. This is not just a theological concept but a spiritual reality that requires us to renew our minds to walk in its fullness.

The signs and wonders Jesus performed were examples of what we are now called to do. **Casting out devils, healing the sick, and moving in supernatural power** are not extraordinary events but part of our normal inheritance as believers. Jesus made it clear in Mark 16 that these signs would follow those who believe, illustrating that the **power to do these works comes from being in Him.** This is not something we do on our own but through the Spirit who empowers us.

However, this **ascension power is not just about miracles; it includes spiritual gifts and ministry offices.** The fivefold ministry—apostles, prophets, evangelists, pastors, and teachers—exists to equip the body of Christ to walk in this power. **When these gifts function as they should, the Church grows into the fullness of Christ, reflecting His glory and authority on earth.** Unfortunately, many believers remain unaware of this truth because it is not often taught. This omission has allowed the enemy to gain an advantage, as many Christians fail to exercise their authority in Christ.

The ascension gifts were given to the Church to equip believers for the work of ministry and to build up the body of Christ. **Each believer has a role in manifesting the fullness of Jesus on earth.** This means understanding the gifts of the Spirit, such as prophecy, healing, and tongues, which are manifestations of the Spirit's power. **These gifts are not optional but essential for living a victorious Christian life.** They enable us to discern, act, and speak with divine authority, bringing Heaven's will to earth.

One of the first acts of Heaven after Jesus' ascension was to send the Holy Spirit. **The Spirit empowers us with supernatural knowledge, ability, and language, equipping us to live out the ascension reality.** The same Spirit that rested on Jesus during His ministry now dwells in us, enabling us to do the works of God. This truth challenges us to step out in faith, knowing that the results are not up to us but to the Spirit working through us.

Many believers hesitate to operate in this power because of fear or a lack of understanding. **Fear of failure often paralyzes us, but we must remember that we are not the source of the power; we are merely vessels.** Our job is to obey and act in faith, trusting that the Spirit will manifest His power as needed. This mindset liberates us to step out boldly, knowing that the responsibility for results lies with God, not us.

The Spirit's manifestations, such as words of wisdom, knowledge, faith, and healing, are tools for building up the body of Christ and advancing the Kingdom of God. **These gifts remind us that we are co-laborers with Christ, empowered to bring His will to pass on earth.** They are not reserved for a select few but are available to every believer willing to yield to the Spirit's leading.

Finally, the ascension power calls us to a life of faith and action. **We are seated with Christ for a purpose: to destroy the works of the devil and to bring the Kingdom of God to earth.** This is our inheritance and our assignment. By embracing this truth, we step into the fullness of what it means to live as sons and daughters of God, reflecting His glory and power in every aspect of our lives.

REFLECTIVE QUESTIONS

1. How does understanding your position in Christ change the way you approach spiritual battles?
2. In what ways can you begin to step out in faith and operate in the gifts of the Spirit?
3. What fears or doubts have held you back from fully embracing the ascension power?
4. How can you support the fivefold ministry in equipping believers to walk in their spiritual authority?
5. What practical steps can you take to build your faith in the reality of ascension power?

ACTIONABLE STEPS

- **Cultivate**: Spend time daily meditating on Scriptures that affirm your position in Christ and the power available to you through the Holy Spirit.
- **Equip**: Seek to understand and develop the spiritual gifts God has given you, whether through study, mentorship, or prayer.
- **Engage**: Act on opportunities to demonstrate God's power, such as praying for the sick, encouraging others, or sharing the Gospel boldly.

Journaling Prompt

Reflect on a time when you felt prompted to step out in faith but hesitated. Write about what held you back and how understanding your ascension power might have changed your response. Commit to trusting the Spirit in similar situations in the future.

~

CHAPTER 15
KINGDOM ESTABLISHMENT

The beauty of the ascension is that it not only revealed Jesus' supremacy but also extended that authority to us. When Jesus ascended, He brought all things in heaven and earth under His dominion. Ephesians 1 shows us this purpose: that we are now a part of His divine plan to establish the Kingdom of God on earth. When I reflect on this, I am in awe that Jesus' exalted position makes us exalted ones through Him. We are now called to function from this position, not from defeat but with authority.

"And He put all things under His feet, and gave Him to be head over all things to the church, which is His body, the fullness of Him who fills all in all." Ephesians 1:22-23 NKJV

When you begin to see yourself as seated in heavenly places with Christ, your perspective changes. **Our new identity as spiritual kings requires us to think and act like rulers.** This isn't about earthly kingdoms or physical rule; it's about reigning over the enemy and establishing spiritual dominion. The resurrection brought us into oneness with Christ, granting us both union and privilege. To live out this calling, we must understand and embrace the **theology of reigning,** or "Reignology," as one of my ministry friends aptly calls it. We have been raised to rule, and it is from this place of authority that we must live.

The concept of reigning in life isn't just a lofty idea; it's a reality Paul urges us to step into in Romans 5. Through the abundance of grace and the gift of righteousness, **we are called to reign in life through Jesus Christ.** This authority is not for the future alone but for now. The battles against spiritual forces are fought and won here on earth. **Jesus' resurrection and ascension were not just demonstrations of power but invitations to participate in His victory.**

Yet, reigning isn't automatic. The enemy seeks to keep us bound in division and ignorance, for a **divided Kingdom cannot stand.** Satan understands this principle and uses it to his advantage, keeping his forces united in their destructive goals. In contrast, the Church often struggles with division, weakening its ability to manifest the Kingdom of God on earth. But Jesus gave us the solution: where the Spirit of God is active, the enemy's power is broken.

The Kingdom of God is established wherever we cast out the works of darkness, declare the authority of Jesus, and enforce the justice and judgments of Heaven. This isn't just a spiritual exercise; it is our mission as those seated with Christ. Isaiah 9 foretold the increase of His government and peace, and that prophecy reaches its fulfillment as we take our place in advancing His Kingdom.

The apostles understood this calling, as seen in the book of Acts. These ordinary men—fishermen, tax collectors, and others—became extraordinary vessels of Kingdom power because they were willing to align themselves with the risen Christ. They healed the sick, opened prison doors, and preached the gospel with authority, not because they were special but because **they functioned from their exalted position.**

This same calling extends to every believer. You may not preach from a pulpit, but you are a vital part of the Church's mission. **Every joint must supply, and every believer has a role in building up the body of Christ.** Division weakens us, but unity empowers us to push back the gates of hell. Jesus made it clear that the enemy cannot prevail against a united and Spirit-filled Church. Our unity, combined with the power of the Holy Spirit, makes us an unstoppable force.

The ascension wasn't just for Jesus' glorification; it was for our employment. We are exalted for a purpose: to **bind and loose, cast out devils, and bring Heaven's will to earth.** When we declare, "Thy will be done on earth as it is in Heaven," we are not merely reciting a prayer but affirming our role as enforcers of God's Kingdom. This is our assignment. This is why we are seated with Him.

Reflective Questions

1. How does understanding your seated position with Christ influence the way you view spiritual battles?
2. What does it mean to you personally to be part of God's mission to establish His Kingdom on earth?
3. In what areas of your life can you begin to exercise spiritual authority more effectively?
4. How can the unity of believers strengthen the Church's ability to push back the gates of hell?
5. What steps can you take to align your daily actions with your heavenly position?

ACTIONABLE STEPS

- **Cultivate**: Spend time daily meditating on Scriptures that affirm your identity as seated with Christ in heavenly places.
- **Equip**: Seek teaching and mentorship that deepens your understanding of Kingdom authority and your role in God's plan.
- **Engage**: Take intentional steps to exercise your authority, such as praying boldly, declaring God's promises, and standing against spiritual opposition.

JOURNALING Prompt

Write about an area in your life where you've struggled to see victory. Reflect on how understanding your seated position with Christ might change your approach. Commit to stepping into your authority and documenting the outcomes as you align with God's will.

CHAPTER 16

RELEASING THE HEAVENS OVER YOUR LIFE

Even when we were dead in trespasses, God raised us up together with Christ. This is the reality of our spiritual position: though we live physically on earth, we are spiritually seated in heavenly places. This dual reality defines Kingdom living and unlocks the mystery of the authority we have in Christ. Jesus gave us a glimpse of this dynamic in His teaching on prayer, encouraging us to call upon the Father in Heaven to release His will on earth. He revealed that our blessings are allocated from Heaven, and it is through prayer that we align the realities of earth with the dominion of Heaven.

"Thy kingdom come. Thy will be done on earth as it is in heaven." Matthew 6:10 NKJV

The power of prayer is not merely a request; it is a declaration that **Heaven's authority overrules earth's circumstances.** When Jesus prayed, He demonstrated the connection between Heaven's authority and earthly change. Through His prayers, the dominion lost by Adam was restored, and complete authority was reestablished on earth. This heavenly authority was evident from creation when God spoke over the earth, and it obeyed. Adam, as God's representative, exercised this divine dominion, naming animals and stewarding creation. **This same authority has been restored to us through Christ's ascension.**

Jesus taught His disciples persistence in prayer, urging them to ask, seek, and knock with faith. **This persistence is not about begging but about unwavering confidence** in God's promises. If God would not withhold the Holy Spirit, the greatest gift, He will surely provide everything else we need. We pray not as desperate petitioners but as partners with God, releasing Heaven's will over our lives and circumstances. This partnership requires faith, as much of our communication with God happens in the unseen realm.

To truly release the heavens over your life, you must **abide in Christ** and align your desires with His will. Jesus said, "If you abide in Me, and My words abide in you, you will ask what you desire, and it shall be done for you." This abiding positions us to discern His will and speak it into existence on earth. **The promises of God are already yes and amen in Christ,** and we declare them in faith, knowing they are accomplished in the heavenly realm.

Victory on earth is maintained by staying in the seated position with Christ. **Satan cannot access this position unless we allow him to through fear, doubt, or disobedience.** Quick repentance and a commitment to Kingdom principles ensure that the enemy has no foothold in our lives. Remember, Kingdom promises are tied to Kingdom principles. You cannot claim the blessings of God while living in contradiction to His Word.

When you release the heavens over your life, you become a vessel of God's will on earth. Prayer becomes more than a spiritual exercise; it becomes an act of governance, aligning your life and circumstances with the authority of Heaven. This is your inheritance as one seated with Christ, and through faith and obedience, you can bring Heaven to earth in every area of your life.

REFLECTIVE QUESTIONS

1. How does your understanding of being seated in heavenly places with Christ change the way you approach prayer?
2. In what areas of your life do you need to release Heaven's authority and align with God's will?
3. How can persistence in prayer deepen your faith and confidence in God's promises?
4. What steps can you take to ensure you are living in alignment with Kingdom principles?
5. How can you partner with God in prayer to manifest His promises in your personal and intercessory prayers?

ACTIONABLE STEPS

- **Cultivate**: Spend time daily meditating on Scriptures that affirm your position in heavenly places with Christ. Reflect on Ephesians 2:5-7 to renew your mind to this truth.
- **Equip**: Identify promises in Scripture that relate to your current challenges and begin declaring them over your life with faith and authority.

- **Engage**: Actively release Heaven's will in your prayers by aligning your requests with God's Word, speaking with confidence, and resisting fear and doubt.

Journaling **Prompt**

Reflect on an area of your life where you've struggled to see change. Write a prayer declaring Heaven's will over that situation, affirming God's promises, and aligning your faith with your seated position in Christ. Document the results as you persist in prayer and faith.

CHAPTER 17

YOU HAVE THE ADVANTAGE

The Spirit is your unparalleled advantage, sent to guide you into the ascension dimension of life. Jesus emphasized this when He told His disciples it was better for Him to leave so the Holy Spirit, the Comforter, could come. The Spirit's role is not to adapt to your natural level but to elevate you to a spiritual level where divine mysteries and wisdom are revealed. Through the Spirit, you gain access to the mind of God, which the natural mind or the enemy cannot comprehend. This is the foundation of living victoriously in Christ.

"But as it is written: 'Eye has not seen, nor ear heard, nor have entered into the heart of man the things which God has prepared for those who love Him.' But God has revealed them to us through His Spirit." 1 Corinthians 2:9-10 NKJV

The enemy cannot contend with the Spirit of God or with those operating in the Spirit. **Satan's blindness to the resurrection underscores the limitations of his knowledge.** He remains a perversion of his former self, stripped of authority and understanding of God's wisdom. In contrast, the Spirit searches the deep things of God and imparts revelation to believers, giving us unparalleled insight into God's plans and purposes.

Living in the ascension dimension requires more than intellectual understanding; it demands an active relationship with the Spirit. **The Spirit communicates God's mysteries directly to your spirit, bypassing natural reasoning.** This divine communication includes speaking in tongues, a language of the Spirit that allows you to connect with God beyond human limitations. As you pray in the Spirit, mysteries are revealed, and God's will becomes clear, giving you strategic guidance in every area of your life.

Through the Spirit, you are empowered to navigate weaknesses and limited knowledge. **He intercedes for you with divine precision, ensuring that your prayers align with God's perfect will.** As you yield to Him in prayer, He orchestrates all things to work together for your good. This partnership with the Spirit is central to the ascension dimension, where the supernatural becomes a daily reality.

A Spirit-filled life is foundational to experiencing the fullness of ascension living. **You must create an environment where the Spirit can thrive, making your life a sanctuary for His presence.** This requires living in holiness and walking in alignment with Kingdom principles. The Spirit is grieved by sin and quenched by neglect, so maintaining a vibrant relationship with Him is essential.

Your inheritance in Christ includes both eternal promises and present blessings. The Holy Spirit ensures that you access the down payment of Heaven on earth. **Meditate on the realities of unity, victory, authority, and royalty that are yours in Christ.** These truths are not just for the future but for now, enabling you to reign in life with Christ. Your redemption, forgiveness, righteousness, and adoption are the foundation of this incredible inheritance.

To fully embrace the ascension dimension, you must prioritize spiritual disciplines. **Daily engagement with God's Word, prayer, worship, and walking in love will keep you connected to the Spirit's power and guidance.** These practices are not mere rituals but pathways to experiencing the supernatural life God intended for you.

Living in the Spirit is not about occasional experiences but about a consistent lifestyle. **You were redeemed and seated in heavenly places to manifest God's Kingdom on earth.** The Spirit is your guarantee, ensuring that you walk in the fullness of your inheritance. Never forget that your position in Christ is your greatest advantage. Guard it, cherish it, and live from it every day.

REFLECTIVE QUESTIONS

1. How does the presence of the Holy Spirit change your understanding of your spiritual inheritance?
2. What steps can you take to create a life that is a sanctuary for the Spirit?
3. In what areas of your life do you need to yield more to the Spirit's guidance?
4. How can praying in the Spirit deepen your connection to God and reveal His will?
5. What practical changes can you make to prioritize your spiritual disciplines and live in alignment with Kingdom principles?

ACTIONABLE STEPS

- **Cultivate**: Spend intentional time each day praying in the Spirit, allowing Him to reveal God's will and align your heart with His plans.
- **Equip**: Study Scriptures that highlight your spiritual inheritance in Christ, such as Ephesians 1 and 2, and meditate on these truths until they shape your mindset.
- **Engage**: Create a daily routine of worship, prayer, and meditating on God's Word, ensuring that your life becomes a sanctuary for the Spirit's presence.

JOURNALING Prompt

Reflect on the areas of your life where you feel limited in knowledge or power. Write about how the Holy Spirit can guide you into deeper understanding and breakthrough. Document your prayers and revelations as you actively partner with the Spirit to release God's will over your circumstances.